Following A Special Star

Mary and Joseph traveled to a town,
Looking for shelter, a place to lie down.

The innkeeper said, "There's no room tonight."
"Sleep in the stable until it is light."

So Mary and Joseph went in to stay,
Next to a cow and a horse eating hay.

With only the animals standing near,
Miracle of miracles did appear.

Into the world, Mary's Son came,
Born in a manger, Jesus His name.

The angels came with tidings of joy,
Singing a song for the new baby boy.

The shepherds were filled with feelings of cheer,
They went to the boy, the Savior was here!

Then into the stable came three men so wise,
They brought the new baby a lovely surprise.

The King of Kings this child will be,
"We followed the star bringing gifts of three."

"Frankincense, myrrh, and bright shiny gold.
The birth of the Christ child we did behold."

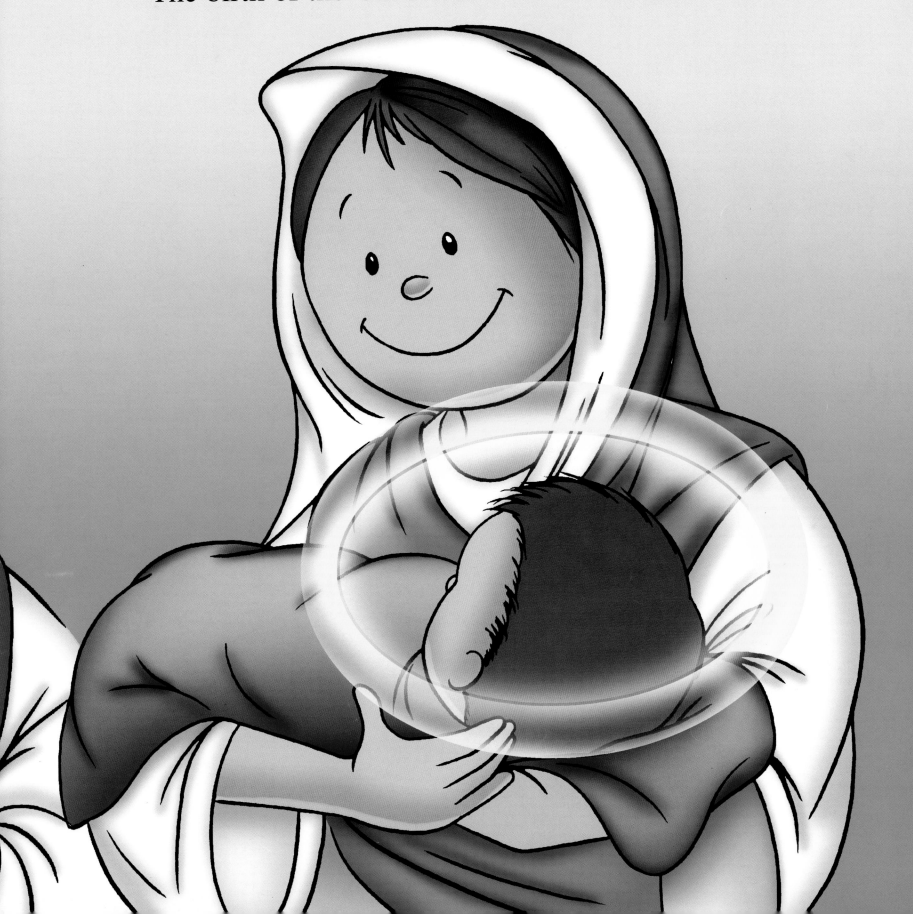